Little
Savage

D0931986

Little Savage

EMILY FRAGOS

with a Foreword by

RICHARD HOWARD

Grove Press
New York

Published simultaneously in Canada
Printed in the United States of America

FIRST EDITION

Library of Congress Cataloging-in-Publication Data

Fragos, Emily.
    Little savage / Emily Fragos
        p. cm.
    ISBN 0-8021-4065-3
    I. Title
PS3606.R345L58 2004
811'.6—dc22   2003060717

Grove Press
841 Broadway
New York, NY 10003

04   05   06   07   08   10   9   8   7   6   5   4   3   2   1

For my mother

Contents

PART III

Foreword
A Note on Emily Fragos's
Little Savage

You are alone in the room, reading her poems. Nothing is happening, nothing *wrong,* but all at once, say around page 17 or 18, you hear—remember, no one is with you, no one else is there—a sigh. Or a whispered word: *someone.* You are not alarmed, but you had thought you were alone. Perhaps not. The sensation is what Freud used to call *unheimlich,* uncanny.

That is the effect of the poems of Emily Fragos. Like their maker, her readers are *accompanied,* and not to their ulterior knowledge. It is not disagreeable to be thus escorted, attended, *joined,* but we had not expected it. And as Robert Frost used to tell us ("no surprise in the writer, no surprise in the reader"), Fragos too has not expected such visitations, as she will call them. This poet—these poems—endure *otherness,* they are haunted:

"I remain, with one of everything." "Even as one is being saved . . . conjure the army of others" "What would happen to my life when all along there has been nothing but me?" "Did you not see how I was made to feel when you put me among others" "And my body—uninhabited—suffers and wonders: whose hands are these? whose hair?"

The poems will reveal whose, though I do not think Emily Fragos herself ever finds out. Inevitably, we recall that old surrealist shibboleth, "Tell me by what you are haunted and I will tell you who you are"; it can be the password to identity. But this poet has what she calls "luxurious mind" and her ghosts are legion:

> Alone in my odd-shaped room, I practice
> blindness and the world floats
> close and away. I am uncertain of
> everything. I must walk slowly, carefully.

She is acknowledging, with some uneasiness ("will you please tidy up?"), that it is not only the beloved dead, the proximate departed who are *with* her, who possess her, but others, *any others*. The remarkable thing about this poetic consciousness is that the woman's body is inhabited—sometimes with mere habitude, sometimes joyously, more often with astonishing pain—by the prolixity of the real (and of the 'unreal'); the poems are instinct with *others:*

> How dare you
> care for me when all my life
> I have had this voltage to ignite
> me, this rhythm to drive me,
> when something inside your body
> dares me to touch my hands
> to yours . . .

And quite as remarkable, of course, is the even tonality of such possession; there is nothing hysterical or even driven about the voice of the poems as it records, as it laments or exults in these unsought attendants. There is merely—merely!—a loving consistency of heedfulness; and one remembers Blake's beautiful aphorism: *unmixed attention is prayer.*

Of course such poetic staffage is not peculiar to Emily Fragos; like Maeterlinck, like Rilke, she exults in her discovered awareness: "I need the other/the way a virus/needs a host." Rather, she imbues, she *infects* all of us with the consciousness that there are no single souls: we are not alone.

Richard Howard

Where should this music be? i' th' air, or th' earth?

—Shakespeare

I

Apollo's Kiss

Devise Cassandra. Become her, in possession,
And the world becomes perfect. For even gods
Crave perfection. Desire her like a man
And like a man be refused in all your desire.
Surrender: beg a first and last kiss and pray
She will acquiesce, her virtue stirred.
Then, breathe into her mouth the powered
Prophesy and for all you are losing
—the deprivation she will give and give—
Release her half gifted, as you are, half mortal.

In the courtyard, animals are captured
By their hind legs, held up on haunches,
Throats slashed. She walks on burning
Stones. Swift, it is slaughtering season.

Pompeii, A.D. 79

The day before, as there is always that
completed day with all its hours intact,
we drew blackened water from the well, threw
stones at the birds shrieking in the sky.

The last night in our beds, you will remember
our dreams: warm mouths swollen with sleep,
soft eyes closed, trapped somewhere else.
We did not get far on foot. The trinkets

and bracelets, the mice-covered vases
you have carefully dusted and preserved,
we carried in our hands. Our children, gathered up
naked in our arms, clutching at our necks.

You will imagine our face as the fire overtook us,
sliding under our feet at a little past noon.

Il Maestro del Violino

*Those afflicted with incurable diseases would go to the
Incurabili, founded in Venice in 1522. There, hundreds
of abandoned children were provided with music lessons
and were taught to perform at mass and at vespers.*

Somewhere behind the huge thick doors
        deep within the bowels

of the Incurabili on the Zattere a long
        paved street facing

the Giudecca and named for the rafts
        that unload their wood there

we live until we die and are taught
        our lessons by Maestro

Mateo Puppi who plays violin by day
        and composes admirable

sonatas by night of full harmonious
        music for us to play.

Sweet-faced angels he calls us and
        once a lovely man

he called friend with hair the color
        of carrots and eyes as green

as Chiaretta's parrot came to hear
us play his concerto

and pronounced us marvels of great
facility and expression.

Signor Vivaldi patted me on the head
and sparkled like a star

so bright in the sky that he
turned night to day.

Those of us still pretty enough
to leave give concerts

in the open air and return to tell
of shrieking gulls and

large faces and the warm breeze
that blows across our

bare legs and arms as thin as reeds.
Francesca conducted our

chorus with sound flowing like water
the light glinting off

this voice and then off another.
When she died, I played

my instrument in a monotonous frenzy
all high-pitched and piercing

and made Him hold his ears in pain.
        My cat Gatto is fat

with the rats he catches every day
        strolling about the dark

halls with a skinny tail hanging
        from his mouth.

One by one we pass away and are buried
        under signs in the garden

behind. We can see the markers from
        our windows and speak to our

friends who listen from above. We
        appear only as first names

and the instruments we played: Francesca
        del coro, Luciana organista,

Luciete della viola, Anna Maria and
        Silvia del cello. Me, I am

Sofia del violino. Once I saw myself
        in a clear puddle of rain

water. My teeth are very crooked, I
        know. We are none of us

startled by the other. We are all
        the same. To Heaven.

Mondays

Every village has its lunatic,
its talking parrot, its spot in the park
where lovers lie between two trees.

At the post office,
there she is, pushing her carriage
filled with garbage, her head a poodle
of ludicrous yellow curls.

She tells her Bengali doctor:
I don't know how long
it's been out there on the lawn,
but it's not dead yet.

He looks back at her
with liquid eyes
and speaks in spurts,
which makes her nervous,
makes her want to open
her mouth, sing opera.

She rushes from the clinic,
through the park, sees
the lovers sitting up, the round red blossoms,
the ink-black blossoms.

At the veterinarian's, the parrot
is being handed over for lung surgery
and calls out: *Come here.*
I love you. I want to go home.

Medieval

There was only a thin strip
of fantasy. I traced its patterns
in my bare feet, my gypsy bracelets
clicking at my wrists. It never
wore out—you on one end—
a body in blue adagio.

The chords reminded me of everything
sensual I loved. Now the cello
is put back in its huge human
case and stands voiceless
against the bedroom wall.

Tomorrow I will cart it
downstairs into the streets
filled with the curses of plague.
The children will throw stones.
The bronze bell will sound.

Tomorrow I will carry you
downstairs into the clutter
for the festive insane to sleep inside.

Glenn Gould, Dead at 50

It is darker where I am.
I cannot tell, holding my hand
over one eye, if it is female there.

At six,
I multiplied endlessly
and began to feel close
to sacrifice.

The music took root
inside, like torture,
all tension, ritard, release.

It is in every part
of my body now, and there is not
room left for me.

I have burned
all my capes, got rid of my papers.

Graces

Your son gives you a ring to wear and you wear it.
Thalia and Melpomene, identical masks with inverted mouths,
the little faces on your fourth finger you stare at

when he is gone and you mourn, moving about the rooms
of your expensive home in a bruise, touching your fingers
to his shoes, his clothes, his hairbrush on the bureau.

It is rude to leave messages that do not get answered,
your friends tell you. Walking about like a ghoul, they say.
They crush you with their extravagance for grief has made you
simple and one glance: *But this has nothing to do with manners.*

I imagine you turning a corner, a bag slung over your shoulder,
rushing to meet him at the door of the schoolhouse
and only this matters: the metal ring on your finger,
raising matching cups to your lips in soothing synchrony.

The Art of the Insane

The good Doctor Prinzhorn says it was the patent
that snapped me in two like a twig,
that shattered my lovely personality, so to speak.
I nod my heavy head.

Have you seen my machine, perpetually moving,
whirring, breathing? Made it out of cloth
and mud and dirt and spit and excrement.

Dear Diary: Dubuffet and Klee came last week
to copy my faces. Eager to meet me, touching
my creatures with their long, skinny fingers.

They smeared my orange chalk, calculating
what they could steal. . . . And if anyone asks,

I am taking my pig Rafi for a walk.
With her hooves of long curls like a little girl's
mop, or Persian slippers, excellent for flying,

we are wind gone. We are kingdom come.

The Prodigy Paints

From inside her arms and legs,
the wild monkeys quiver and twist,
open their mouths.

She can feel their heads, their nails
scratch at the inside of her skin.
Their panicked eyes stare out
from behind hers.

It is moments and hundreds
are born. They shove
each other to escape
from being lost.

There are walls for them
to climb and ceiling and flesh
and the smooth inside
of a young girl's mouth.

There, the invisible seizure,
and her brush is stopped
in midair; a tail, claws, and half
a head are caught in the end,

maniacally frozen, hearing
our whispers—

the posture, the pressure,
the breathing, the breathing. . . .

Logic

I started smoking again after a long time
without. I don't remember why I lit up:

some envy, some fear I could not face. Went
to the corner and bought my brand and took it

up so easily in my hand, my mouth, I could
not imagine not ever performing this fluid

motion. It tasted bitter and my head
was dizzy but I kept at it until it changed

to smooth forgetfulness and warmth filled
my lungs. Fresh air was slim and common

compared to this, beautiful darkness.
And gone the enormity of quitting, how it was

suddenly always this powerless sweet hunger
so strong I wondered how I never ended up

with needle marks in some shooting gallery,
with dirty clothes and dirty hair, some

mountain-heavy man on top of me. It was
easier to imagine than me on some campus

with books in my arms taking notes with
a black felt-tip pen. Now I am up to two

packs a day. I can feel my body collapsing
as I walk the streets. I can feel people

staring at me, uncovering all my secrets
in broad daylight. Eventually I will have

to start thinking about stopping all over
again. And keep in mind this time what they

always say: Watch out for false highs;
there is another person with your eyes,

hair, and mouth on the other side of the room
whispering *hurt thyself, starve,* and it

will seem the perfectly right thing to do.

Velocity

I once outran my own body
like the sprinter accelerating down the track
until the point reached within
when he can no longer be contained
by this world or be impeded
by these limbs.

And he must come to full stop
pulled up and dissolved
into pain on the track.

I once wanted someone and no one else
and yearned and turned
my body inside out and still
I could not have my desire.

It grew and like a monster
split in two
and each half grew and strained
and split in four
and my body could not hold
this gathering.

I woke from wild-eyed dreams
with tired legs incapable of flight.
I woke with a delicate retina
detached in the vanishing light.

Visitations, but None Come

Flightless bird
ravenous on dust
for sustenance.

Little savage
taking its revenge at will
with stopped-up mouth.

Ugly feet
pick up dry sticks
like poems

pen clenched
between prehensile toes.

Host

There are two worlds I know of:
the vast illumined
and the place where I am.

I need the other
the way a virus
needs a host,
but the strange,
loving sisters
hold up their hands.

And my body—
uninhabited—
suffers and wonders:
Whose hands are these?
Whose hair?

II

Antarctic Night

I have found a job writing letters,
long and puzzling, on pale
pink stationery, for the woman
with glass eyes.
She speaks serenely
from a distant place as my hand sways

down the page—antarctic night,
luxurious mind. Will you please
tidy up? she asks, when it is time
for me to leave. The money
is placed in piles, the letters sorted

by colors she touches and sighs.
Alone in my odd-shaped room, I practice
blindness and the world floats
close and away. I am uncertain of
everything. I must walk slowly, carefully.

Dissonant Fugue

My hyacinth mother beside me
on the piano bench, her hand
touching the notes
on the page, as I took them in
like rapture in spirals
weaving my breath.
And where they flung me,
I followed, wondering what I would
have become without music,
without my hyacinth leaving me,
too early and after too much suffering.

Emily of Amherst

The sherry-colored eye drifts
inward: not metaphor,

but botched in Boston
where the surgeon

—not knowing what vision
he was twisting,

what mind
behind the face he was touching—

pulled at the roots
like a farmer

and left you
(brother mother

sister starved) in
white despair.

A Sacrifice

The sky so blue and the sun white
with rage blistering you. Your mother
helps you bring the cup to your lips
and taste the sweetest water. A smile
that has never been more beautiful
or more pure, the last depth of expression.

How much, Iphigenia,
this is killing us, from centuries
apart, sending us out
into the world like wounds,
while your wide eyes
breathe in the light and know
nothing of your helplessness
or ours: how the pain swells
like heat all around us.

The Escape

Why are those men dipping their hands
in yellow paint and leaving palm prints
around the gunwale of their boat?
Has the sun burned holes in their brains?
Where do they think they are heading
in that rickety little skiff
on this water of stony silence?

Is it that boat being towed, the sky obliterated
in thick mist, with its five shrouded
faceless passengers—one tiny figure,
I swear, must be a child,
or dwarf—oarlocks creaking?

If I run along the shoreline, hiding
behind the bodies of trees, I can follow
until I see what I am seeing.
Strangely, I belong to this boat and its cargo now,
even as I hear my name being called,
tangled in the branches above me.

Michelangelo in the Marble Mountains

In the marble mountains, a wild and violent man,
at once no different than the two servants who skittered

behind him in annoyance and exhaustion, surged and sculpted
his shapes in the air. They must have heard his abrupt fall

to the ground and the spiraling up from gnarled knees,
the twisting torso and open howling: *I will sculpt a mountain!*

Watched as he scooped earth out with his hands and flung
it into his pail with a clang. And when they helped him

home again, the windows were just windows, plates of glass
in cupped wooden frames. They must have supped together—

three glasses of red wine, some meat—and felt the sad
    voluptuousness
of too muchness, which they tried to describe. But that could not

have been what he intended, he must have whispered, for it was all
so absurd, these things they were telling him, so strange and pained.

Star Pharmacy

White-jacketed, fluorescent lit, without bed,
he tends the insomniac, panic-attacked, migrainous,
and occasionally cut. There, he points out,
just below the jawline, the jugular pulses.

The infant's ceaseless crying on small sheets,
the insane stamina of a mother's grief—he scoops up
colored capsules like a solemn boy at play, and eyes
the cooling elixirs in their miniature bottles.

The welcoming bells chime a minuet.
There is ranting in the middle aisle and respite
from about—earth slowly revolving and no one falling off.

While You Slept

The crows, with a soft, astonished flush,
lift from their branches, as no living thing without wings

can get about. There was a great fire
in the city while you slept: fire engines, hoses,

torrential gushes of water looped through open
smoking windows. From the roof, screams and hands

reaching up and down. Ladders all the way to heaven
as one at a time bodies were lowered and others

remained. Someone hurled himself like a mounted acrobat
from a ledge into the empty air. Sirens wailed in the distance.

Face

The girl said the landlady was deranged,
had slapped her, set her German shepherd upon her
for no reason on the street. Her voice

was odd and marvelous. What could I do, call her
a liar? Such a plea for sympathy
and attention. And perhaps, I wondered,

it was true, after all, the claim. Out on the sidewalk,
the landlady was walking the dog, a curious old
creature sniffing at the end of a leash.

I glared when she greeted me and passed
in silence. My face is freezing;
not like the girl's, though, with those eyes and mouth

that change blue and shape like a dancer
who can erase each figure with the next,
making space for forward only.

Solstice

Did you not see how I was made to feel
when you put me among others?
Why did you not show sympathy
for my brooding,
my gruesome jealousies? Why show me
him and her, saying: See
how they play with one another,
how much they trust their soft bodies
to my touch, how they place their gloved hands
into each other's and swing themselves
into the snow?

With a stick I drew stick faces in the hardened
ground, touching my people
with the long, cold finger,
rubbing the lines so they turned to crust
and weathered away like the oak
outside my window.

I watched them through the river
and stuck my hand into the icy water;
watched their reflections shake and quiver,
hoping they would disappear into the depths,
as you, scented and looming, never would.

A Small Fine

The book from the library
was overdue and with fifty-odd pages left,
and the penalty of a small fine,
I returned it, watched the librarian

pull out the manila card
and throw *The Loser* atop a pile of books.
This man has lost everything
he ever wanted and now he wants

a bullet in the mouth.
On the way home, I buy the book.
I put the loser on the highest shelf
and keep him dusted, facing the window.

I am beginning to hear him move
about in his chair, craning his neck
to get a glimpse of me. I hear him
scratching his fast-growing beard

and cracking his huge knuckles.
I make him wait on the white
page between his covers. I let
him grasp what outlives him.

The Cat Show

Fastidious judges with dainty hands
disinfect tables; disease must not be spread.
The cats await examination, bred
for showing, their coats caressed and muzzles scanned
for perfect proportion, roundness, balance, brands.
Oblivious and docile Persians are led
from cages: ribboned, groomed, prudently fed.
One judge tries to trick them, flicking peacock strands.
The crowd feels shabby, awed by nature's ways:
the finish, fullness, panache and drapery;
massive and slender, peaked or pug bodies;
refined intelligence, lioness be praised.
The priestess cat is held on high—sacred.
This contest claims victory for gifts from God.

For the War

Birds with human eyes
beg me to feed them
Leaping from the trees
emptying out the sky
they rush to land
in flocks at my feet

My father refused
to feed the birds
stale bread
He would sit on a bench
and eat it himself
for the Depression
he said for the war

That is why they come
with human eyes
and dive from the trees
and beat down the sky to find
me They know whose child
I am and what I hold

Cri de Coeur

What if you said yes
to everything. What would happen
to me then. I am telling you
the rage would start and never
come to end. How dare you
care for me when all my life
I have had this voltage to ignite
me, this rhythm to drive me,
when something inside your body
dares me to touch my hands
to yours. And if you said go
ahead, touch. What would happen
to my life then, when all along
there has been nothing but me.

In Margins

I bury my harm
in margins of woven nests,
aisles of unreadable texts,
feathery edges of pillows,
mother's sad sepia photograph
(a child poses solemnly).

Everything I cement together
like a frenzied animal,
winter and hunger approaching.

Sonata

In memory of Jacqueline du Pré (1945–1987)

The wind is picking up, so unexpected
    for this time of year, and such
        dissonance in the air.

Ecstasy is simple, you see. The light
    fills my waiting hands. I touch
        music to breathe and beauties

Grow from our strangest wounds. Dust
    scatters from room to room and
        lands now on my bow

So heavy I strain to lift it. And if
    I do not draw my bow
        there is no sound.

These quakes, these tremors, surely
    they come from the center
        of earth. My head will not

Stop shaking; breasts grown huge
    pull me down, my fingertips
        can feel nothing.

Rest, you say. Lie down quietly.
  It is only your nerves,
      your exquisite nerves.

The Path

There is so little to go on: a pale
trembling hand as I stand over you,
my finger tracing the words on the page,
a foreign language you are learning
for a journey without me. You will do
fine, I say. You will wrap your tongue
around these sounds and be understood,
be given what you desire: a loaf of bread,
change for your money, an antique doll
with violent eyes. Paintings are hanging
on walls, behind glass, waiting for you
to admire them. Their plaintive beauty
will move through you and you will walk
back to your hotel through the park
I know well. I spent years there walking
its bridle path, a gray cat in my arms,
moving toward you, blind, in another life.

III

The Vermeer Lady

The light just misses you entering the room.
It falls in the corner where nothing lives.

If it landed on your slender, stooped shoulder,
your long neck; warmed your dark hair,

your quiet face, you would cringe and the pupils
would shrink like a scream and draw you

back to the fire coals of the cave, the stale air
you breathe, the wet bread shoes of the forest. The world

just outside, its dazzling squawks of birds
upon birds: let them come to you as echoes, as whispers,

the vocalizing of meek and clenched creatures
you have never seen, the flat-faced owl with whom,

for an instant, you merge. With inexhaustible fingers,
thrifty and nimble, slip the thread through the primitive

needle and piece together your fabric. If they come,
it is only to collect your goods and to give you

something small in return: a loaf, a beeswax candle,
perhaps, to delight you. You can see in the dark

by the pinprick in your eye. It is the point where
all thought dissolves, the purifying corridor of enigmatic

links. Light its wick in the night and see what ignites.
If you were to speak, might it not kill you?

Harvest

A woman with huge ears is stirring a kettle with a shovel
while out in the endless fields girls in gray bonnets and aprons

strain for hours to shake branches down. Fruit is bruised;
    the dredging
of water pots over blistered shoulders to the plowmen
    with restless hands

and someone is always being whipped, always being entered.
    So many children
in rough clothes, chasing the chickens, the pigs, the yoked oxen,

the tethered birds, the wide-eyed donkey with his birch bundles
and pulled logs. A sword disappears and reappears from out
    of a dark mouth,

a snake is charmed; a boy's body sways with the power
    of the bloodied palms.
In the yellow fields, the lute, the lyre, the sweet pipes. Two figures

in red hats, until the trees erase them. Someone being bedded
in cool white sheets, someone dark-crowning from between

long legs, someone blowing on the soup. Loose bodies are sinking
into the sod, the skin sloughing off her beautiful face,
     the bothered bones

assembling. The fisherman sitting in the quiet and the fish
     gasping
next to him. The end of the story is the end of expectation:
     the door

that stays closed, the sound of shatter, a rush past, a breeze,
     a dry cough.

Velásquez Dwarfs

They must have been about, collecting at his feet,
as he carried his easel and paint bottles and brushes
into the lady's posing room. She, he could tell you,

is beauty, quietness and amplitude conjoined, her spaniel
cuddled in her lap, the ring on her—exquisite.
The white lace collars climb like spiders up their necks

and at their cuffs velvet blouses and brocade jackets
tiny enough to fit the pet parrot in. He is looking
for her visage in everyone else's and finding *them,*

their trays of hot tea and sweet cake, their mild blue eyes
and hydrocephalic heads tottering and thick. *What is gone
and cannot be got back.* Between the pose and the paint's freeze

is flesh and a slash of red as dazzled as grief. How we float
in fragility like a small fish that when provoked
has a voice both watery and gravel.

The Drowned

Even as one is being saved, pulled by the sopping collar
from an ivory ocean, limbs quivering, and bundled

by sturdy hands in green blankets, conjure the army of others,
having fallen out of rocking boats, having swum

too far, after the sudden ankle-pull under, after the astonished
plunge, the soft twig-crack of extinction—how solemnly

they drift away. And even as the rescued one, frigid hands
rubbed pink, air bursting like lilac sachets in the lungs,

is roused to land, a foreign feeling in the legs,
they open and shut their mouths like sullen fish,

making precise, pathetic gestures with their frozen fingers,
going deeper and out farther, even as through a pond's

diaphanous patch, a gloved hand hovers to remove another,
skates still laced at the feet, from their mute presence,

moving still behind closed, curved eyes, inside strange skin.

Company

I've lost my stately others and now there is me with neck
erect and solemn, tightened face. Sometimes I feel they are
peering out from behind white curtains, clutching with long

arthritic fingers the edges of chenille, wiping their mouths
as after a succulent roast or giggling like ninnies in the pantry.
Once I turned, but it was only a wisp of my own dark hair.

I wanted them gone for so long, world devised of nothing
but me, distractionless, pure, but I was wrong. Me is empty
as wilderness, air—no monarchs, no moths.

Callas in Hamburg

Who says it is beautiful, that middle range, lies—
for it is not, nor is it meant to be. Full of dust-
choke and nebula-bound sky, you slide

into her realm, colorless and brittle-toned
as the sound of a spoon banging the burned underside
of a copper pot, where the highs and lows no longer

bear the sayable: how tightly wrapped bodies
come unraveled in the dark and a distance
sets in like a spell of stillness that, when broken,

could harm. You do not remember your dreams
here, for excess is no longer energy but murder
with bare hands. There is no chance of sleep

either; even closed eyes stare mesmerized and all
you can pray for is languor and distraction,
a woman spinning slowly, then wildly in air.

In the Egyptian Museum

The light and taunting voice, so filled with wild embellishment,
grows heavy, without shine, and sinks to the bottom of the pool.

Trees behind long windows stare in—somber, disciplined—
old women with gnarl in their bones and a patience for clouds

and the sullen glares of the malcontent. The deaf schoolchildren
pick at their lips and sit on marble benches, waiting to be led home

by the hot hand, up narrow steps, and lifting their scented dresses
above their heads, slip quietness on, as devotion commands.

In Memoriam

What lives in the dark humming—not symphony, not divinity,
not the author of her life. It is cooing to her as Othello
coos to Desdemona—as the bawdy nurse to her pretty Susan.

Behind her lies the city in silver and blue sliver. No one sails
on the river of myth; no one holds her breath. A wild bird
is preparing with utmost concentration for its next move,

which will not take place for one million years.
And the spiders, picked up and dropped at will by a gust,
leave their legs behind to dance in the air, spinning on a grief.

Wasps

All in a single stroke, a thousand deaths.

All gone and their stings dead.
No one to warn them, returning to the pit of a tree,

that in one hour or less the killer will put down his hat
and stroll in their direction, holding the poison gun.

Clasp

for Helen

The daylight enters and the birds begin their music.
For those who have left us in the middle of the night, there is

no staunch standing up to go toward the singing, no yawning
of the jawbone, hinged like a necklace, no hard hand

grasp. The long hair slicked with imperturbable dust
is not washed again and piled in a twist, soft and brown,

with only a few strands floating in air. What is slid apart
may not be clasped together; what is soiled by the spiders

will not be made clean. The door flies open only when
a ghost runs through it. The closed window stays closed.

Noah

I could get used to the closed door and windows
and forsake all others in an instant. Years of going forth,

of speaking and drawing others to my body,
are erased. I have got going in the opposite direction

now, and whatever I may need, let it come—and soon,
you'll see, there will be no want of anything more.

All that was familiar is suddenly odd. As if a flood
had washed it all away. I remain, with one of everything.

Alchemy

You were frozen inside my hands. I could not touch
for fear of being touched. Now the imperious cat
moves toward me as if to say *enough;* she sniffs

the rug where you stood offering gifts and, bored
with your scent as I am fed up with your death, chases
the frantic fly up inside the yellowed lampshade,

where it bangs and bangs its head away. I feel the edges
of my body, the dance, with its screams and jitterbug leaps;
I open my mouth and bees fly out. I never expected this.

Sorrow

She is small-boned and shy, offends us by her silence.
We wish to make her real until she arrives like a guest
and won't pack her foul-smelling clothes or stop stealing

our cherished possessions. The candelabra went first,
smashed to crystal bits in a childish fit of rage, a snit
because we happened to be out of peanut butter. She put

the pet ferret's tiny tail in the rat trap in back of the fridge
and totaled our new Toyota. On Saturday night, sorrow's
robed in a cranberry dress and sports a huge gold buckle

at the belted waist. She draws compliments all around
for her upswept hair and false lashes, her large anemone
eyes set wide apart, and the high forehead, a sign

of intelligence. She folds her legs at the lovely knees.
My mother and sister are arriving for Christmas, sorrow
squeals. Sorrow has a sister! Put the cat on top of the tree

instead of the star, the sorrow-child laughs, and how like
our unlike mothers we emerge to become. Sorrow hasn't
brushed her teeth or hair in centuries. We put pen and paper

out for her to write letters with in the middle of the night.
This adds charm to my thoughts, she explains. Sorrow is so full
of herself. The snow saturates her body, cold as a radiator,

and "Can't you turn the heat up, cheapskates? I'm freezing!"
she screeches from the attic, where she goes to dance. Long
after we are in our beds, tired heads upon the world's pillows,

you can hear the thumping and pounding of her long feet,
tapping at the ground like a palomino. The stalky elegance,
the pointy toes of sorrow. We have not slept in years.

Hall of Records

The birth occurred in the morning and the doctor's name
was Italian. There was no catastrophe of mindless proportion

in Quito, Ecuador, that buried thousands alive in a river of mud.
Neither was it boiling out but simply mild, for you have checked

the newspaper's headlines for that day. The president
did not call in troops to keep peace among the rioting looters.

The police never did catch that murderer who left the girl
child behind the schoolhouse, one shoe off and never found:

a trophy he retains in an old trunk stowed under his bed.
At night he takes them out—left shoe, charm bracelet, barrette—

to touch and smell. His name is not John. The two brown horses
tethered to the riding pole were grazing in the field when the boy,

dreaming of Sarah, threw his smoke into the stall and walked away.
He did not hear the horses stirring, did not write a bad love song,

practicing three chords on a cheap guitar well into the night.
There is no Sarah. A woman once again on that day failed to call

the boiler repairman; he never took the toothpick from his mouth
to fix her eyeglasses with, where the little pin had fallen out.

Increase of Appetite

Scrawny and pallid creatures taken pity on and bought
from the store while the chartreuse and royal-blue parakeets

had to be left behind; but then, the guilt of having left them
prompted a renewed excursion to other stores and other birds:

parrots with torn feathers and cracked beaks, cockatoos turning
grim yellow at the chin, even pigeons, standing frozen on the city

sidewalks, carried home half dead inside newspapers while riding
on crowded buses and kept in shoe boxes on the bathroom floor

until they died inside. (I bury them in the park at night. There are
ordinances against it.) My life is not my own. I spend my time

feeding them, scooping out seed of one kind or another, vitamins,
antibiotics, with little bird spoons and replacing their bowls of water

and cleaning up after them. I put covers over their cages but you
don't know owls with their rotating heads and nightingales that sing

in the dark—lovely music but not lulling really. Not satisfying,
not compatible in a human way. Most mad-screech and
 nasal-whine,

blurting out *peter peter* or *phoebe phoebe* all hours of the day.
They become despondent and won't leave their cages, looking
    out at me

as if to say, *But what is my crime, sir, that you keep me here?* Now that
people hear the cacophony, they give theirs or what they find,

but what do they do but overwhelm one who is already
    overwhelmed!
You do not know. They have their own rules and deaths
    and routes

to follow—there above the darkening trees, there along
    the hushed river,
there where no one yet has traced them to an Andean
    mountaintop

like the Monarchs all gold and black and silently drumming.
If the food runs out, if the winter cold freezes them to the hollow,

if there are those who fall behind or drift from the pattern from
    weakness
or bad eyesight, the perils of predation, and fall away,
    irretrievable—

A million sorries I say to the birds; a million sorries they sing
    back to me.

The Scarlatti Sun

The mute seamstress on her knees
sticks a pin in the hem
and weeps for the cloth;

the dead stop their dying,
their heads warming like stones
in the Scarlatti sun,

while the grave postman,
his worn leather bag strapped to his back,
feels his mind go, windswept.

An old woman at her window,
her old cat on the sill, sips thick coffee
from a saucer, and in the shuttered convent,

the novitiate, taken up,
rushes across the just-washed floor,
daring the ground to break a bone.

Snow Land

Whatever is false, white-gloved Winter raves, remove!
Monarch a woman with closed mouth and mournful expression,

a face devoid of human adoration. She will ride across the steppes
on a copper-colored horse, his great mane flying, and speak

what she means or remain devoutly mute. We will feel the breath
as it comes from our nostrils and become as wounded animals,

unaware of anything but the ache in our hips and limbs. Suffering
will teach us Spring and the spare melodies of the slender bone flute.

The Other Place

Long lines move quickly to their destinations and all the notes
    of the minds
are a disappointment compared to this. Here the sounds
    unravel at a new speed

and new memories are created each instant, an accretion of
    cathedrals
that leave the face flushed and permanently amazed. Rest your
    bothered bones

in preparation for this place; fathom those moments of solemn
    quiet or restlessness,
as when the cat who touched your feverish sleeping face with
    her paw

cried out like a child. Here even those on four legs no longer
    fear abandonment
for they have spotted your beautiful form in the glass as you move.

Acknowledgments

The author would like to thank the editors of the following publications, where some of these poems (a few in earlier versions) first appeared: *The American Voice:* "Il Maestro del Violino"; *Barrow Street:* "Mondays"; *The Boston Review:* "Logic," "The Vermeer Lady," "Hall of Records"; *Chelsea:* "Apollo's Kiss," "Pompeii, A.D. 79," "Medieval"; *Columbia:* "Clasp," "Noah," "Alchemy"; *The Pacific Review:* "Sonata"; *The Paris Review:* "Company," "Callas in Hamburg"; *Parnassus:* "The Scarlatti Sun"; *Salonika:* "Emily of Amherst," "For the War," "In Margins"; *Southwest Review:* "The Drowned"; *The Threepenny Review:* "The Path"; *The Yale Review:* "Harvest"; "Apollo's Kiss" appeared in *The Best American Poetry 1998,* guest-edited by John Hollander; "The Violin Master," "The Art of the Insane," "Velocity," and "The Path" appeared in Poet's Sampler of *Boston Review,* Vol. XXII, Number 3–4, Summer 1997; "Glenn Gould, Dead at 50" appeared in the anthology *Northern Music,* John Gordon Burke Publisher, Inc., and was reprinted in the magazine *Piano/International Piano,* May/June 2002, in a review by Benjamin Ivry.

To Lucie Brock-Broido, Richard Howard, and Marie Ponsot with deepest gratitude. Special thanks to my sister, Elizabeth Faranda, for her invaluable support and assistance in the preparation of this manuscript. Sincere appreciation to Joan Bingham, Lindsay Sagnette, and Michael Hornburg of Grove Press for making this book possible.